D0653003

the way of
f**k it

the way of
f**k it

small book. big wisdom.

John C. Parkin & Gaia Pollini

Australia • Canada • Hong Kong • India
South Africa • United Kingdom • United States

First published and distributed in the United Kingdom by:

Hay House UK Ltd, Astley House, 33 Notting Hill Gate, London W11 3JQ

Tel: +44 (0)20 3675 2450; Fax: +44 (0)20 3675 2451; www.hayhouse.co.uk

A catalogue record for this book is available from the British Library.

ISBN 978-1-84850-156-0

Printed in the UK by TJ International, Padstow, Cornwall.

*Dedicated to the growing army
of F**kiteers around the world.*

Contents

F✗✗k it

TEICUT IS, !

JOHN

FON THE

BOOK

CHISENE

FOEU

FUck it

When we said we were going to write another book, Leone made some initial sketches.

3.

Introduction

The rather beautiful process of putting this book together has been one of continuous simplification. Now, it is difficult to throw out ideas. So we had the idea a while back of writing an introduction that talked about the process of throwing things out, and also referring to some of the things we threw out... That way we'd trick ourselves into thinking we weren't really throwing them out. You see? The mind's a tricky blighter: you have to keep it happy in one way or another.

One thing about keeping things simple: I remember that the acronym K.I.S.S. was commonly used in PowerPoint presentations some years ago. K.I.S.S. means Keep It Simple, Stupid (I think that comma was necessary, otherwise it could have read 'Keep it Simple and Stupid', and that probably wasn't the point). Now I love the sentiment, of course, but did the person who invented it have to use the word 'stupid'? Why did he (and I assume it was a 'he', I'm afraid) have to be so insulting? If a woman had written it, I suspect it would have been K.I.S.S., Keep It Simple, Sweetheart. 'Oh sure', I'd respond, 'thanks for the advice, I'll really try.' Instead of my rather more alpha response to the original Keep It Simple, Stupid: 'Don't call me stupid, or it'll be outside for you'.

Anyway, this process of simplification also neatly mirrors the whole process we've gone through with F**k It. Reaching the realisation that this profanity can create profound change in our lives, and can actually constitute a spiritual process… would this realisation have been possible without the 20 years of serious study of meditation and Eastern philosophy, without the struggle for answers and clarity? Who knows. But what's for sure is that F**k It supplies for all of us a wonderful, practically miraculous, shortcut to liberation in our lives.

Maybe this is a simplification too far, but I would suggest that this very Western profanity sums up all of the best Eastern wisdom. It does so because it – quite uniquely in our (Western) language – contains the implicit suggestion that things just don't matter as much as we think they do. In two words, we realise that our problems arise because we take things too seriously, and that letting go of this seriousness, this sense of things mattering so much, can create liberation and change in our lives. This is what the Buddhists were going on about with all that stuff about attachment and suffering. It's true. It can just be hard to get your head round. Whereas F**k It is not. We all know, instantly, why F**k It works to create more freedom in our lives.

So you can do the same in your life as we've done in ours, with the process of F**k It and of this book: sure, you can study all the Eastern philosophy too, read all the self-help books, do all the therapy, but keep bringing it back to the basics, the simple. And there's no better way to do that than with F**k It.

So have a look here at some of the drawings we played with (and threw out), including some of the boys' (who, rather beautifully, always refer to this idea in their heavy Italian accent as

'fook eet').

What we've left you with in the end is the idea at its purest: quick powerful ideas as to how to use F**k It in your life, every day.

Read the book through from front to back if you want. Or use it by opening randomly and finding what's right for you at that latter process works miraculously, cards, providing you with the right exactly the right time.

moment. The like divination message at

One thing together: it's (rather than the looking out over the

about the process of putting this book been a joy to do everything together usual process of writing alone...), sitting hills wondering how to illustrate each idea...

always pushing each other to better and better ideas (which often included responses like this, only possible between man and wife: 'No, that's totally rubbish, what about this?'). It's been great.

We've ended up with something we love, and, with the help of our supportive and inspired publisher, Hay House, we're getting it to you in exactly the form we wanted.

And we have to say, as that's not such a common ex-creatives in the media, outcome, believe us.

So, please, get stuck in. the magic of F**k It in your soon enough. So, we'll say of keeping it simple, true and start to unleash the magic of Open and start to unleash life. And it is magic, you'll see it again, in the hallowed name powerful: Please open and F**k It into your life.

Pause… Later...

Okay, so we wrote that introduction on the plane back to Italy. Returning home we found that Arco, one of our boys, had done a drawing for this book… and look at it (opposite)… a magician unleasing some 'F**k It magic' (his words) for someone. By gum, this stuff surprises even us sometimes. So it now seems appropriate to open with Arco's magic contribution.

Love,
John, Gaia, Arco & Leone xx

Now begin to unleash the
magic of F**k It into your life.

Say F**k It to your
plan for today.
Open to something
spectacular happening.

Say F**k It and
accept everything
just as it is.

BEAUTIFUL

You don't have to get it right all the time. F**k It.

Do not care what others think of you.

Stop judging everyone and everything.
F**k It. It's just boring.

Say F**k It and refuse
to do anything that
could be done tomorrow.

Say F**k It and eat it.

Say F**k It and buy it.

F**k It. Confess
to a lie you've told.

Say F**k It and contact someone you know you shouldn't.

Say F**k It and open
to the idea that
you'll meet someone today
who could change
the way you see things.

F**k It.
Get a cleaner in.

F**k It.
Get a babysitter in.

Say F**k It and make
a cup of tea for someone
you really don't like.

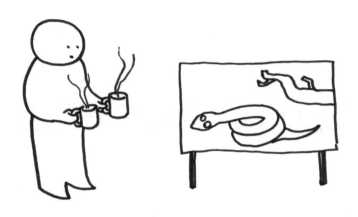

So I'm different. F**k It.

Say F**k It and give the cash in your wallet to someone who needs it more.

Don't compare yourself to others. F**k It.
There are always 'better' and 'worse' people out there.

F**k It.
Stay in bed
until you feel bored.

Say F**k It and get in touch
with your first sweetheart.

Say F**k It and 'shopdrop', placing something unusual you've bought in one shop, in another.

What's the one thing you can't say F**k It to? How would your life change if you did?

Say F**k It
to lost dreams,
and find the dream
in everything
instead.

F**k It. Pack your suitcase, ready to leave at a moment's notice.

Say F**k It and live like you never had to think about money.

If you realised that
it was all an illusion,
what would you do?

Say F**k It and go
on a news-fast
for seven days.

F**k It. Travel first class whenever you can.

Turn this page into an aeroplane
and throw it at someone
you love.

Message brought to you by:

F**k It Air

I love you.

What you believe in becomes true. Believe in something absurd.

Say F**k It and invent
a fantasy job for yourself
for special occasions:
I am a pest controller,
specialising in cockroach
infestations ('they're one of
the hardiest creatures
on the planet, you know').

Say F**k It and book yourself into a hotel tonight.

Say F**k It and watch a movie you know will make you cry.

F**k It. Go to a church
and pretend you're praying.

F**k It. Do the thing today that most scares you.

Say F**k It and buy *The Sun*,
read it in McDonald's
over a kids' Happy Meal.

Maybe you don't need to:
Earn as much.
Achieve as much.
Do as much.
Be as much.
F**k It.

Say F**k It and cancel your gym membership.

You have every reason
not to be happy,
but need no reason
to be happy.

Say F**k It and
play hide-and-seek
with someone.

Say F**k It and
go to sleep
in one of the
beds at Ikea.

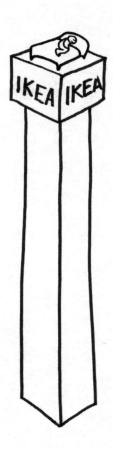

F**k It. Buy the book
the cashier recommends.

Say F**k It to being
a great lover.
Do what you feel like
instead.

Say F**k It and lie down
in a shopping mall.

1. Say F**k It and throw away your to-do list.
2. Say F**k It and throw away your to-do list.
3. Say F**k It and throw away your to-do list.
4. Say F**k It and throw away your to-do list.
5. Say F**k It and throw away your to-do list.
6. Say F**k It and throw away your to-do list.
7. Say F**k It and throw away your to-do list.
8. Say F**k It and throw away your to-do list.
9. Say F**k It and throw away your to-do list.
10. Say F**k It and throw away your to-do list.
11. Say F**k It and throw away your to-do list.
12. Say F**k It and throw away your to-do list.
13. Say F**k It and throw away your to-do list.
14. Say F**k It and throw away your to-do list.

F**k It. Say 'yes' when you'd normally say 'no'.

F**k It. Say 'no' when you'd normally say 'yes'.

You've searched.
You've done the therapy.
You have all the badges.
All this to discover
you were already there.
F**k It.

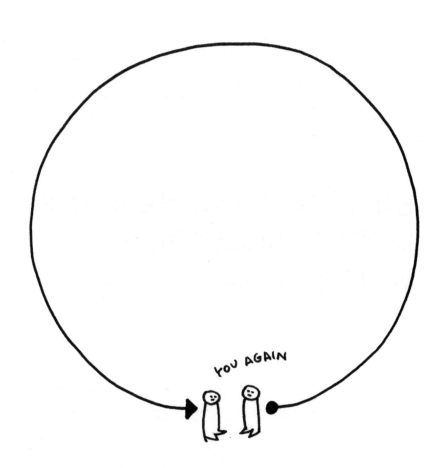

Say F**k It and stand still
in the busiest place
you can find.

Next time you
don't feel like
doing something...
You guessed it.

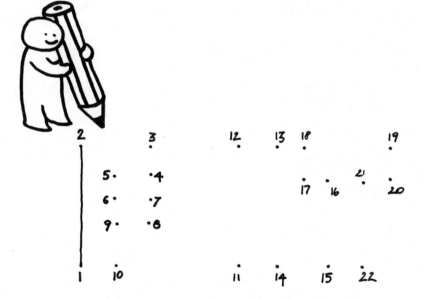

You've been a naughty girl/boy.
You've taken things too seriously.
Write 20 lines, saying F**k It
to all those things.

I say F**k It to...
I say F**k It to...
I say F**k It to...

Say F**k It and throw the scales away.

We've got something amazing to share. But some of you will find it difficult. F**k It, we'll make it even more difficult...

The idea of saying F**k It comes from a radical realisation –
That we are all one and therefore do not exist as individuals –
That the world as we know it, reality as we perceive it –
Is just an illusion – and that everything in this illusion is
Simply an arising of oneness – all, therefore, divine,
All beautiful, nothing good or bad, nothing better or worse,
No going anywhere, no point, no meaning,
Just Oneness, unicity, playing with itself,
The Eternally Masturbating God, if you like.
This is very difficult to get. In fact, it's probably impossible.
But it's probably true… all the great religions and philosophies
Point to this truth… all mystics, meditators, visionaries and seers
See the same thing… the one thing.
So, don't bother 'getting it'. Say F**k It for now.
But at least it's been said. And one day it might well be seen.

When things go
wrong, say F**k It
and move on.
No one died after all.

When things go wrong
and someone dies:
Feel the grief fully;
Remind yourself how lucky
you are (for not dying);
Consider the possibility
that death could be
totally fine anyway.

Separation is an illusion.
It takes a good few F**k Its
to see that.

Say F**k It and
catch a train
to somewhere you've
never been before.

Say F**k It and
ask your best friend
what they'd do
in your position.

What you think matters,
probably doesn't.
What you think is real,
probably isn't.
Who you think you are,
you probably aren't.
F**k It, just enjoy yourself.

NOT
WHAT I THOUGHT
I WAS

Say F**k It every time
you feel some pain,
and see what happens.

Just do it.
You don't have to wear
silly trainers that cost too much.
Or start training for a marathon.
But it's a good line.
F**k It. Just do it.

Say F**k It to the goal of happiness. Just doing this will cheer you up no end.

There is no difference between watching the football and meditating.

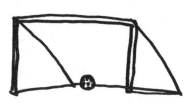

We go, if we're lucky, from life living us (child), to us living life (adult), back to life living us (The Way of F**K It).

F**k It. Invite the Jehovah's Witnesses in for a cup of tea.

Do only what you enjoy.
Enjoy all that you do.
Including having
a great big poo.

1.

Co-written with
and illustrated by
our sons, Arco & Leone,
aged 8.

2.

A journey of 1000 miles starts with a single step.
(But then there are 1000 miles, less a single step, to walk... which is a heck of a long way).

F**k It. You're already there.

Say F**k It and write 'love' in marker over your heart.

Say F**k It and write 'centred'
in marker, just below
your belly button.

Say F**k It and write 'grounded' in marker on both your feet.

Say F**k It and say 'I love you' to someone you've never said it to before.

F**k It. Do the opposite
of what you would normally do
in every way.

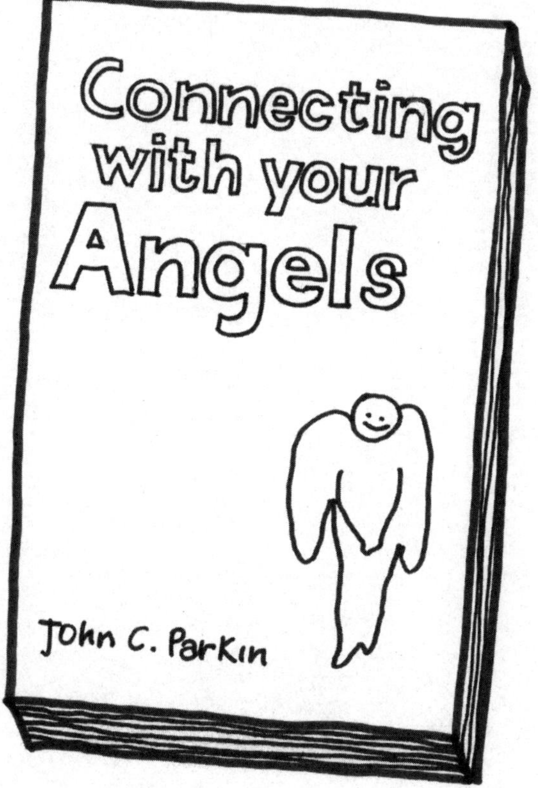
Connecting with your Angels
John C. Parkin

Say F**k it to
excelling at work:
explore the average;
revel in your weaknesses.

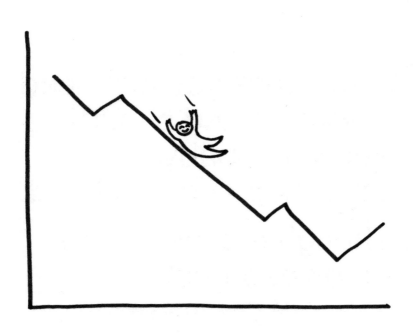

Sometimes you just need
to scream and shout and
blub like a baby.
Say F**k It and go ahead.

(Though maybe not on
a crowded bus).

Some days just don't so well. F***

things
work out
..

F**k It. Don't send any Christmas cards this year. If questioned, say doing so is environmentally unfriendly.

It's a cliché now.
But, F**k It, it makes you think:
Write your own gravestone.

INTERESTING FACT:
When you say F**k It to
anything and trust yourself
or give in to the natural flow
of events, you slip (effortlessly)
into tune with universal energy,
consciousness, the Tao if you
will, and by doing so, as well as
feeling good and looking good,
you start to attract miracles
into your life and might well
find yourself with apparently
superhuman powers.
And that's a fact.

Say F**k It and remember that everything you worry about doesn't matter a jot in the grand scheme of things.

All things manifest from nothing. Leave space, lots of space, in your life.

Say F**k It and place a bet on something you know nothing about.

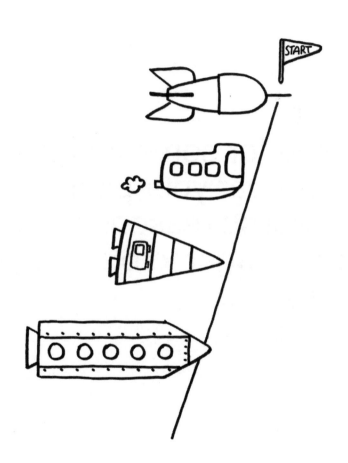

It's time for some therapy:
a. rake over your past.
b. establish reasons for misery.
c. don't forget to blame parents.
d. cry. a lot.
e. pay. a lot.

1.

RAKING OVER YOUR PAST

Or you can say F**k It,
put your feet up,
and concentrate on what is,
not what has been.

2.

LIVING IN THE NOW

F**k It. At Christmas buy the best present for yourself - and ensure you get exactly what you wanted.

F**k It. We're going to teach you
the best thing we've learnt from
30 years of meditation,
25 years of tai chi and qigong,
10 (long) years of yoga,
1000s of books, and
the bloody University of Life:
You don't have to do anything
to be okay.

Get a F**k It tattoo done.
Take a picture of it.
Send it to us and we'll put it up.
(john@thefuckitway.com)

Say F**k It and
Google yourself:
contact the namesake
who comes top.

All pain is created
by attachment.
You don't get that?
F**k It.

Say F**k It and hum
Bohemian Rhapsody
on the Tube, all the way through.

If at first
you don't succeed...
give up.

Say F**k It to being cool

Sometimes the only solution is to F**k It… Him, Her, usually not It.

Say F**k It and leave.

Say F**k It and stay.

You don't have to remember any of this. You don't have to believe any of this. You don't have to apply any of this.

You're always in the right place at the right time.

You know you
don't want to go.
So don't go.

Just be
yourself.

F**k It.
Close this book.
Give it to someone
who clearly needs it.
Buy yourself another one.

Say F**k It to always staying in touch.

YOU'VE READ THE BOOK – NOW GO ON A F**K IT RETREAT IN ITALY

This is where it all started: John and Gaia ran their first F**k It Retreat in 2005.
They're now running these famous retreats in spectacular locations around Italy,
including an estate and spa in Urbino, and on the volcano of Stromboli.
Say F**k It and treat yourself to a F**k It Retreat.

'Anything that helps you let go is okay on a F**k It Retreat.' THE OBSERVER
'I witnessed some remarkable transformations during my F**k It Retreat.' KINDRED SPIRIT

F**K IT
RETREATS

LIVE THE F**K IT LIFE

WWW.THEFUCKITLIFE.COM

YOU'VE READ THE BOOK - NOW TRY A F**K IT ONLINE COURSE
and explore John & Gaia's teaching from anywhere in the world.

We hope you enjoyed this Hay House book. If you'd like to receive our online catalogue featuring additional information on Hay House books and products, or if you'd like to find out more about the Hay Foundation, please contact:

Hay House UK, Ltd., Astley House, 33 Notting Hill Gate, London W11 3JQ
Phone: 0 20 3675 2450 • *Fax:* 0 20 3675 2451
www.hayhouse.co.uk • www.hayfoundation.org

Published and distributed in the United States by:
Hay House, Inc., P.O. Box 5100, Carlsbad, CA 92018-5100
Phone: (760) 431-7695 or (800) 654-5126

Fax: (760) 431-6948 or (800) 650-5115

www.hayhouse.com®

Published and distributed in Australia by: Hay House Australia Pty. Ltd.,
18/36 Ralph St., Alexandria NSW 2015 • *Phone:* (61) 2 9669 4299
Fax: (61) 2 9669 4144 • www.hayhouse.com.au

Published and distributed in the Republic of South Africa by: Hay House SA
(Pty), Ltd., P.O. Box 990, Witkoppen 2068 • *Phone/Fax:* (27) 11 467 8904
www.hayhouse.co.za

Published in India by: Hay House Publishers India, Muskaan Complex,
Plot No. 3, B-2, Vasant Kunj, New Delhi 110 070 • *Phone:* (91) 11 4176 1620
Fax: (91) 11 4176 1630 • www.hayhouse.co.in

Distributed in Canada by: Raincoast Books, 2440 Viking Way,
Richmond, B.C. V6V 1N2 • *Phone:* (1) 604 448 7100
Fax: (1) 604 270 7161 • www.raincoast.com